Drop of Consolation
Spiritual Ascents in the Silence of God

Fr. Christodoulos

Dedication

To you who suffer and feel as though God is silent. To you who spoke to Him in prayer and heard only silence in return. To you who remained faithful without applause, who carried your cross without anyone seeing. To you, I dedicate this book. Because you are not alone. Because His silence is not neglect. It is His way of drawing closer to your soul. And to You, my Christ, Who did not speak—but remained.

TABLE OF CONTENTS

Foreword

I am not writing as a teacher. I am writing as someone who has suffered. Who searched for God through tears and found Him in silence. This book does not aim to explain God to you nor to solve your questions. Its purpose is simply to sit beside you, to kneel with you in the dark, and to whisper: You are not alone. The Words of Consolation are quiet breaths of faith born not when God was speaking, but when He was silent. And then I realized...His silence was not absence, but Presence, testing our love. If even one soul finds within these pages a sigh that resembles their own,a hope they thought was lost, or an answer that has no words, then this book has fulfilled its purpose.

Do not fear the silence of God. For in it, your Resurrection is hidden.

† The Least Hieromonk Christodoulos

CHAPTER 1

When God Is Silent – and I Suffer

"My God, my God, why have You forsaken Me?"

– Matthew 27:46

1. The Silence That Terrifies

There is no pain deeper than the one clothed in silence, not mere absence, but the aching void of unanswered longing. It is the silence of God. The hush of heaven. The stillness that descends like a cloud over a wounded soul. Even the Son of God, the incarnate Word, did not cry out against the nails or the betrayal. On the Cross, He cried only once with a cry that pierced eternity: Why have You forsaken Me?" He did not complain when humans mocked Him. He did not protest when they crucified Him. But when the Father withdrew His felt presence, He cried out—not in rebellion, but in pure sorrow. His cry gives voice to every suffering soul who feels alone in divine silence. And yet, that silence was not a void. It was pregnant with divine mystery. In embracing it, Christ transformed it. He showed us that even silence can be salvific. The absence of words does not mean the absence of love.

2. Where Are You, God, When I Need You?

O Lord, where are You when I tremble alone at night? Where are You when my heart breaks and there are no arms to hold me? When I call out and no answer comes when friends leave, when lies wound me, when the world forgets me, where are You? I remember when I felt Your nearness. Your love once warmed me like a gentle sunrise. But now, it seems as if all light has gone out. I speak into the silence, and only my own echo returns. I feel like a child waiting outside a locked door, hoping for the Father to open but no one comes. And still... something within me knows: You are here. Not because I see You. But because I trust You. Not because I feel You. But because I believe. True faith begins where feelings end. To trust when no signs are given. To love when there is only silence. That is the faith You teach in the dark.

3. The Fathers Speak of Silence

The holy Fathers of the Church never feared the silence of God. They entered it. They dwelt in it. They taught us to see its hidden beauty. Saint Isaac the Syrian wrote: "When God is silent, He is working secretly in the depths of your soul." Saint Gregory the Theologian affirmed: "The silence of God is His purest language—one that only hearts tuned to eternity can understand." And Saint Paisios would often remind us: "When God is silent, He is not absent. He is preparing your soul to long more deeply for His light." This silence is not punishment. It is pedagogy. A school of the heart where we learn to listen beyond sound. Where we trust beyond what we see. Where we love without answers. "I served the Lord faithfully for years," one priest confided.

4. Witnesses from the Wilderness

A Priest's Testimony

"Then, in a single night, I lost both my wife and daughter in a car crash. I fell into despair. I shouted to God and the heavens were mute. Two years passed in shadows. I doubted my priesthood. I doubted my worth. Then, one frozen dawn, while serving Liturgy alone in a remote chapel, I felt a whisper: 'I am here. I never left.' From that moment, I stopped searching for signs. I began to trust the silence. A Mother's Pain Another soul, a mother who lost her child to illness, shared this: "Every night I would pray through tears. 'Where are You, God? If You are real, speak!' But nothing came. Only silence. Years later, I realized He was not ignoring me. He was holding both me and my child. Quietly. Eternally." These stories do not offer explanations. They offer companionship. They teach us that the silence of God is often His most intimate embrace.

5.   When Understanding Fails

There will be days when our minds cannot comprehend our suffering. When all prayers seem lost in a desert wind. When we are emptied, stripped bare before the mystery. In these hours, God does not explain Himself. He does not say, "This is why you suffer." He only says: "Believe." Job lost everything: family, health, security, and yet God gave no clear reason. His silence led Job to a greater awe, not a clearer answer. God's silence is not weakness. It is sovereignty. It invites us not to understand, but to surrender.

6.   Faith That Endures the Silence

The truest faith is not that which rejoices when miracles appear. It is the faith that endures when nothing happens. Saint Silouan the Athonite passed through fifteen years of what he called "abandonment." And yet, in that very darkness, he heard Christ whisper: "Keep your mind in hell and despair not." To believe in the silence, to love in the void, to walk when there is no light that is the mark of a saint.

7. The Silent Strength of the Virgin

At the foot of the Cross, the Virgin Mary stood silent. She did not shout in protest. She did not collapse in despair. Her Son was dying before her eyes, and she said nothing. But her silence spoke. It said: "I trust." It said: "Even now, I stand with Him." Let us learn from her. To pray with our presence. To stand with courage. To weep without losing hope. In her, the Church sees what silence looks like when it is full of faith.

8. The Gift of Human Silence

We fear silence because it feels like loneliness. But in God, silence is communion. Saint Augustine wrote: We surround ourselves with noise, thinking it will fill the void. But only when all distractions fall away can the soul finally hear. "In the silence of God, we are truly formed." Let us not be afraid when God does not speak. Let us listen harder. Love deeper. Trust longer.

9. Psalms That Speak for Us**

When we can no longer pray, the Psalms pray for us. "Out of the depths I cry to You, O Lord!" (Psalm 130:1) "My strength fails me, and the light of my eyes is gone." (Psalm 38:10) "In You, O Lord, I take refuge. Let me never be put to shame." (Psalm 31:1) These verses are the cry of every wounded heart. They teach us that we are not alone. That suffering is not meaningless. That silence can be sacred.

10. A Prayer in the Silence**

Lord, I do not ask You to explain everything. I do not need thunder, nor signs. I only ask: stay with me. Do not let me walk alone in the dark. Strengthen me when I falter. Hold me when I collapse. And if You choose silence, Let Your silence be warm, that nourishes. His silence is not punishment. It is invitation. A silent whisper in the soul says: "Will you remain with Me even when you feel nothing? Will you love Me without the comfort of My voice?"

CHAPTER 2

God's Silence as an Invitation to Love

"God's love does not make noise. It approaches quietly, secretly, like dew settling on a flower."

Saint Porphyrios

1. The Quietest of Invitations

When God is silent, He is not pushing us away. He is calling us. He draws us deeper into His heart not through thunder or wonders, but through a silence that nourishes. His silence is not punishment. It is an invitation. A quiet whisper echoes in the soul: "Will you remain with Me, even when you feel nothing? Will you love Me, without the comfort of My voice?"

2. Love Matures in Silence

At the beginning of our spiritual journey, God surrounds us with emotions. The heart burns, the eyes overflow, the soul sings. Later... grace hides. Not to abandon us, but to teach us the art of loving without conditions.

"Can you love Me when I give you nothing in return? Can you trust Mewhen there are no signs or consolations?" When His voice falls silent, what remains is faith. And faith without emotion becomes pure.

3.   The God of the Gentle Whisper

The Prophet Elijah waited for God in the cave. He expected fire, earthquakes, and mighty winds. But God did not come through power, He came through stillness. "The Lord was not in the earthquake...but in a still small voice." 1 Kings 19:11–12

God speaks with the breath of silence. Not to overwhelm us, but to look deeply into our soul. And that can only happen when the world grows quiet around us.

4.   The Fathers on Divine Silence

The saints were never afraid of God's silence. They knew that true love doesn't shout. Saint Maximus the Confessor wrote: "When God is silent, His love is speaking. Words may communicate, but silence unites." Saint Isaac the Syrian reminds us: "Don't assume God has forsaken you when He is silent.In those moments, He is holding you in His deepest embrace." And Saint Porphyrios gently teaches: "We do not always notice when God is holding us because He does it quietly, humbly, and in secret."

5.   A Priest's Testimony – Years Without an Answer

An elderly priest once shared:

"For the first years of my priesthood, grace surrounded me. I felt alive at the altar. Then... came silence. I prayed and nothing. No signs. No answers. Until one day, I realized: That silence was His way of saying, 'I am here.'He was not absent. He was maturing me. And I loved Him not because He spoke, but because He remained. Quietly. Faithfully. Silently."

6.   Silence as Spiritual Formation

God is not a man. He does not speak to entertain or explain. He speaks to shape the heart. Like a father letting go of his child's hand to help it walk, so God steps back so that we might learn to walk by faith. His silence becomes the space where love is tested, where we are no longer led by feelings, but by the decision to trust.

7.   When Even the Virgin Mary Was Silent

At the foot of the Cross, Mary said nothing. She did not scream. She did not protest. She stood. And her silent presence became a participation in the salvation of the world. She loved without asking questions. She shared in the Cross not by speaking, but by remaining.

8.   The Sweetest Kind of Silence

God's silence often defies explanation. But it holds presence. He may not speak, but He remains. He may not perform wonders, but He upholds the soul. He owes us no answers. And yet, He is always near. And that... is enough.

9.   A Dialogue Between the Soul and God

- Lord, why are You silent?

- Because I want you to love Me, not out of habit

- But out of choice. -But I'm afraid of the dark...

- Do not be afraid. I created the night. And I can fill it with light when the time is right.

- I cannot bear not to feel You.

- And I cannot bear being far from you. But this

silence draws you closer.

- So... You are here?

- Always.Even when I am silent...I Am Here.

10. Psalms for Silent Seasons

"Out of the depths I cry to You, O Lord." Psalm 130"Truly, You are a God who hides Yourself." Isaiah 45:15"My God, my God, why have You forsaken me?" Psalm 22:1 These sacred words echo from hearts that once knew silence, too and remind us that even silence has a voice.

11. A Prayer in the Silence Lord

I do not ask You to speak. I ask only that You remain. I no longer need voices only presence. If Your love is silence, teach me how to hear it. If Your voice is hidden, let Your light speak within my heart. Hold me, O Christ, in the silence, and teach me to love You like the saints without conditions.

Amen.

"The kind of love that needs no words is the deepest kind. And when God is silent, He loves in a way that only God knows."

Saint Isaac the Syrian

CHAPTER 3

The Soul That Learns to Listen

"When the soul is silent, it hears God. When it speaks, it hears only itself."

— Saint Arsenius the Great

1. The Inner Stillness That Makes Space for God.

It is not enough to ask God to speak to us. We must learn how to listen. And for His voice to be heard within, all the other voices must fall silent: the voices of thoughts, of judgment, of memory, of pain, of anger, of despair. The soul must become still a silence within. God speaks not with words, but with presence. He speaks through peace, through a tear, through an unexplained awareness in the heart. Often, He does not speak when we beg Him to, but when we become quiet enough to receive Him.

2. Hearing with the Heart, Not the Ears

Saint Isaac the Syrian writes: God does not rest in many words, but in a pure and quiet heart." God's voice is not something captured by ears. It is perceived by the heart. It is not that God is silent but that our inner radio is too full of noise: memories, traumas, fears, desires, expectations. If the soul does not fall silent, it cannot hear anything except itself.

3. Silence as a Deeper Form of Faith

Silence before God is not emptiness. It is prayer at its deepest level. It is the moment we stop asking Him to act, and simply stand before Him like a child who trusts and waits. Saint Silouan the Athonite once prayed for years without hearing a word. And then, one day, without visions or voices, he felt a deep peace descend within him. That peace was the answer. God was not absent. He was simply silent and fully present.

4. Testimony: A Confession in Silence

A priest once shared this story: "A young woman came to confession. She couldn't speak. She just cried. I didn't pressure her. I said nothing. I just stayed beside her, in silence. Ten minutes passed. And then she looked at me and said, ' Thank you. You listened to me more than anyone ever has.'

And yet I had not spoken a single word." The soul listens most deeply when it no longer needs to explain itself to be understood.

5. The God Who Waits to Speak

God never interrupts. He listens to our worry, our panic, our endless words. But He waits to speak until we have fallen silent. When our words run out, His silence begins to speak.

6. A Personal Encounter with Stillness

Once, I stayed in a monastery seeking stillness. I spoke to no one. No phone. No books. Just the icon of Christ before me and the Jesus Prayer repeated quietly on my lips. I heard no voice. I felt nothing miraculous. But on the fourth day, something changed: a gentle stillness entered my soul. A quiet depth. A kind of rest. It was as if God whispered, "Now... now you can finally hear. Because you've stopped having something to say."

7.   Testimony: The Silent Cry

An elderly woman suffering from cancer once told me: "Father, I no longer pray with words. I just picture Him holding me. That's enough. In that silence...He tells me everything I need to hear without saying anything." Pain teaches the soul to fall silent. And in that silence, a new kind of love is born, a love without words.

8.   Dialogue Between the Soul and God

- Lord, I want to hear You.-Be still, and My silence will speak.- But You're not saying anything!- I speak before thought. Before language.- How will I understand You?- When you stop trying to understand Me,   you will begin to feel Me.- And if I forget You?- I will still be there. Because I never leave, even when you do.

9.   Spiritual Practice: The Prayer of the Heart

The Jesus Prayer is not a formula to make God respond. It is a tool to cleanse the inner space, so that the soul becomes quiet enough to receive Him. Saint Symeon the New Theologian wrote: "Learn silence and through it, you will taste the Word." We don't say the Prayer to get an answer. We say it to become habitable for silence.

10. When God Speaks Without Words

God doesn't speak only in prayer. He speaks in a child's gaze ,in a sudden encounter, in a letter, in a silent tear. The soul that has learned to listen recognizes Him even in what has no voice.

11. A Listener's Prayer

Lord, Teach me to be silent not out of fear or indifference, but out of reverence for Your Voice. Teach me to quiet my heart, to speak only when necessary, to think only what the soul can carry. Grant me the art of inner listening: to hear You before You speak, to feel You before You appear. And if I become overwhelmed by thoughts, send me a little divine silence to clear the depths of my soul again. Amen.

CHAPTER 4

God Behind the Sorrow

"Do not be surprised that you suffer. It is there that Grace is born."

— Saint Isaac the Syrian

1. The Shadow of Sorrow

Sorrow feels like a shadow. It surrounds us, weighs on us, darkens us. And yet... no shadow can exist without light. Behind every sorrow, Grace is hidden. Not always as deliverance. Not always as miracle. But always as Presence. God does not abandon us in pain. He hides inside the wound, and in the moment we feel most alone, He is waiting.

2. Sorrow and Prayer

When sorrow comes, we often fight it. We pray for it to leave, for things to change. And when they don't, we think God is silent. But prayer is not a magic wand. It is a relationship. And in the deepest relationships, words are not always needed.

3. The Heart That Softens

The Fathers teach that God is often more present in sorrow than in comfort. Because sorrow softens the heart, it makes it humble, real, and open. Saint John Climacus writes: "Pain is a holy furnace, and God is the Goldsmith who purifies the soul there."

4. God Does Not Send Sorrow

God does not cause sorrow. He does not punish with pain. But since we live in a broken world filled with sin, sorrow becomes part of life. And God does not stay away He enters it, and sanctifies it. He turns sorrow into a place of divine encounter.

5. The Grace of the Cross

Christ did not avoid the Cross. He could have, but He chose not to. He embraced sorrow so that He could walk with every sorrowing soul. And through His Cross, He showed us that Resurrection comes through the wound. Grace passes through suffering. And the Cross becomes a vessel of Grace when we offer it back to God.

6. A Mother's Testimony

A mother had lost her child. She didn't want to live. She wept every night before the icon of the Virgin Mary. I once said to her: "It's okay to cry. Crying is prayer." She replied, "Father, nothing comforts me. But something keeps me going. I don't know what..." I said:" What keeps you going is not a 'something'. It is a Someone. He's behind the sorrow you don't see Him, but He is there."

7. Held by Silence

Some time later, she said to me: "Christ didn't comfort me with words. He held me with His silence. And I understood I was never alone. He never left. He was just there... behind my tears." Sometimes, the strongest comfort is wordless.

8. A Theological Light

Saint Gregory the Theologian wrote: "See sorrow as a mystery, not a curse. It is there that the majesty of God hides."

Sorrow doesn't always make sense.

But it can be transfigured when we live it with Christ.

9. Dialogue Between the Soul and God

– Lord, why do I hurt so much?– Because now I can go deeper into your heart.– I can't take it anymore!– Yet now, you hold on to Me more than ever.– Where are You?– Behind the pain. Inside the Cross. At the depth of your wound.

10. A Prayer in Sorrow

My Christ, I don't ask You to take the sorrow away. I ask You to be inside it. If I must hurt, hold me so I don't harden. If I must bend, strengthen me so I don't complain. If I must walk in darkness, make my heart a lamp of prayer. And when all things fall silent, remind me that behind the shadow, You are shining. Amen.

11. Final Word

Saint Nicodemus the Athonite said, "God is not absent from sorrow. He stands behind it, silently, waiting for you to turn to Him."

That is the mystery of sorrow: Behind every darkness, there is Light. And behind every tear, there is a God who waits Theological Depth A Test of Faith Saint Macarius of Egypt writes: "When prayer happens without consolation, it becomes a sacrifice." And Saint Isaac the Syrian says: "Do not seek pleasure in prayer; hold on to prayer as you would a Cross." True prayer doesn't show itself when the soul soars, but when it drags itself forward and stays kneeling, without feeling anything.

A Personal Moment

I was kneeling for hours before the vigil lamp. I repeated the Jesus Prayer mechanically: "Lord Jesus Christ, have mercy on me..."No inner movement. Dryness everywhere. Until I thought:– "What am I doing? Just repeating empty words..." And then, quietly, a phrase came to my heart: "You speak, and I listen. You remain, and I am here."

No emotion. No revelation. But a quiet certainty was born within me: Christ does not leave just because I feel nothing. He stays – silently, faithfully.

Dialogue of the Soul with God

– Lord, I feel nothing in prayer.– You are praying? That's enough for Me.– I feel like I'm speaking into a void...– Yet I hear you more clearly now.– Am I doing something wrong?– No. Love is measured by persistence, not by emotion.

Prayer in Dryness

My Lord, Today I feel nothing. My heart is dry, empty, weary. And yet... I speak to You. Because I know You are here, not because I feel You, but because You never leave. Teach me to pray without comfort, without reward, simply because I love You. And if I don't come out of prayer enlightened, may I come out more humble. And that will be enough. Amen.

Closing Word

"The prayer made in dryness is heard more clearly because it holds sacrifice."

– Saint Porphyrios

CHAPTER 5

When I Feel Nothing in Prayer

"Hold on to prayer, even without warmth. Faith will heat the emptiness."

Saint Silouan the Athonite

1. When the heart is silent

There are days when you kneel to pray... and feel nothing.

No emotion. No tears. No joy. No presence.

Only a silent stillness unfolding inside you.

And you wonder:

"Am I doing something wrong?"

"Has God left me?"

"Am I unworthy?"

But no.

This dryness is familiar to every soul who truly loves God.

2. Spiritual dryness as a stage

The saints teach us: dryness is not God's absence.

It is a stage. A spiritual education.

God steps slightly back, to see:

Do you love Him without comfort?

Will you stay when you feel nothing?

Will you continue when no answer comes?

3. Patristic wisdom

Saint Macarius the Egyptian says:

"When prayer is made without consolation, it becomes sacrifice."

And Saint Isaac the Syrian adds:

"Do not seek the pleasure of prayer. Hold to it as a cross."

True prayer is not feeling.

It is persistence. Faith. Humility.

4. The silent prayer of God

Christ never promised we would always feel His presence.

But He promised: "I am with you always."

That is enough.

He didn't promise feeling—He promised Himself.

So we don't pray to feel.

We pray because we love.

We pray not to sense something,

but because He is worthy of being sought.

5. A testimony from the soul

A monk once said:

"I prayed for 40 days without feeling anything.

No tears, no light, no warmth. Just exhaustion.

On the 41st day, suddenly fire. Peace. Light.

And I understood: when we fall silent, God works deeply."

6. Prayer without "emotion"

I sat before the vigil lamp.

I repeated the Jesus Prayer like a machine:

"Lord Jesus Christ, have mercy..."

Nothing. No inner movement. No spark.

And then, gently, He came.

A quiet whisper within me:

"You speak... and I hear.

You remain... and I am here."

7. Christ does not leave

He does not depart simply because you feel nothing.

He remains.

Silent. Still. Present. Hidden in mystery.

Many saints felt only darkness, yet they trusted deeper than emotion.

8. A dialogue between the soul and God

- "Lord, I feel nothing in prayer."
- "Still, I hear you."
- "I feel like I'm speaking to myself."

- "And yet you're closer than ever."
- "Am I doing something wrong?"
- "No. Love is measured by faithfulness, not by feelings."

9. When dryness becomes purification

In spiritual dryness, the soul is purified from self-centered demands.

You learn to pray without asking for reward.

You say no longer, "Come quickly, Lord," but:

"I knock... and I wait."

And then He comes silently.

10. Prayer in dryness

Lord, today I feel nothing.

My heart is tight. Empty. Tired.

And yet... I speak to You.

Not because I feel You,

but because You are here.

I pray not for comfort.

Not for reward.

But only because I love You.

And even if I leave prayer not illuminated,

let me leave humbled.

And that is enough.

11. Final Word – A Concluding Thought

"The prayer that is offered in dryness is heard more deeply,

because it carries within it the weight of sacrifice."

Saint Porphyrios

And perhaps the greatest prayer

is the one that continues

even when everything inside you wants to stop.

And yet... you remain.

CHAPTER 6

Silence as God's Pedagogy

"The discipline of the Lord opens the heart of manand makes it a dwelling place of grace."

Saint John Chrysostom

1. When God Doesn't Speak – He Is Not Absent

God's silence is not abandonment, nor indifference. It is a hidden form of presence. Like a father who lets go of his child's hand so they can learn to walk on their own, so God withdraws His felt presence to teach the soul how to walk by faith. Grace seems to depart, but only so that trust can grow.

2. Silence as Pedagogy, Not Punishment

God remains silent not to punish, but to educate us. He is not a vengeful God, but a wise One. Just as a good teacher remains silent during the test, so God's silence means it's time for us to demonstrate our faith, our obedience, and our trust. Silence is His way of forming hearts.

3. Silence as a Spiritual Ascent

Often, grace withdraws so the soul doesn't grow dependent on its sweetness. If a person becomes addicted to the joy of prayer, they risk becoming spiritually soft. God's silence invites us to climb higher, to seek Him deeper, to dig into the roots of faith rather than linger in surface feelings.

4. The Experience of the Saints

Every saint has passed through seasons of divine silence. Saint Silouan the Athonite lived fifteen years in spiritual darkness before Christ revealed Himself to him in light. Saint John Climacus wrote, "He who has never experienced God as absent has never loved Him as Present." The holier a soul becomes, the deeper it tastes this silent pedagogy.

5. The Testimony of a Priest

A priest who had suffered injustice and slander once said, "I cried out to Christ, and He said nothing. I shouted, 'Where are You?' and it felt like He had left me. But in that silence, I matured. I stopped demanding answers and started becoming prayer. I learned to be silent as He is silent. And then, I began to feel Him again—not in words, but in a deep consolation that cannot be explained."

6. Faith That Doesn't Rely on Feelings

When everything is dark and God seems silent, it becomes clear whether we believe in Him because we love Him or just because of how He makes us feel. Faith is not emotion; it is relationship. Not proof, but trust. God tests whether we desire Him, or only the gifts He gives.

7. The Mystery of Absence – Presence

God is both absent and present, like light behind a cloud. We don't see Him, yet He illumines us. We don't hear Him, yet He covers us. Every silence of His is a secret act of care. Every distance is a divine hand shaping us gently through pain so that His image may be revealed in us.

8. The Soul's Complaint – and Grace's Touch

There are moments when the soul cries out, "Why are You silent, my God? Why have You left me?" And heaven seems quiet. But later, the soul looks back and sees: during the silence, God was carrying her. His silence was a deeper kind of voice. His absence was the most tender kind of presence.

9. The Cross of Silence

Christ Himself, on the Cross, said little. He didn't cry out against the pain or the cruelty but against the silence: "My God, My God, why have You forsaken Me?" There was no answer. Yet out of that silence came the Resurrection. Those who remain faithful in the silence of God will one day witness the dawn of His glory.

10. Spiritual Growth in Silence

God's silence is a vault of hidden grace. Like winter that seems barren but nourishes roots beneath the soil, so the soul grows during times of dryness. When we feel nothing, understand nothing, and receive nothing, then often we are being changed the most. God does not always work on the surface, but in the depths of our being.

11. Prayer and Dialogue with God

Prayer Lord, when You are silent, do not leave me. When I cannot hear You, touch me. When I do not feel You, stay hidden within my heart. Do not abandon me, even if I think You have gone. Hide Yourself in my faith. Carve Yourself into my silence. Make my wound Your throne and my pain a prayer. Amen.

Dialogue of the Soul with God

– My God, why don't You speak to me anymore?
– Because now you're learning to hear Me with your heart.
– But I feel empty...
– You had to be emptied so I could truly fill you.
– I feel alone...
– My child, I am now closer than ever
– And Your silence?
– It is the veil that covers you
—until you see Me with the eyes of faith.

Concluding Reflection

God's silence is not punishment, but invitation. Not absence, but a different kind of presence. Just as the sun still warms behind the clouds, so does His grace work within the seeming silence.

So do not be afraid when God is silent. He is teaching you something. He is shaping you, forming you, deepening you. You may feel alone, but in truth, you are never closer to Him than when you walk in the dark holding only faith.

When He is silent, it is your turn to speak not with words, but with trust. Not with questions, but with endurance. Learn to pray not just to hear Him, but to entrust yourself to Him.

For the deepest knowledge of God comes not through answers, but through silence.

And there, at the edge of your patience, a soul is born not one who loves Him for what He gives, but for the mystery of His Presence in the very heart of His absence.

CHAPTER 7

The Trust That Endures the Emptiness

"True faith is not found in the one who sees, but in the one who waits and remains even when they see nothing."

— Saint Isaac the Syrian

1. The Emptiness That Frightens

There comes a moment in the soul's journey when everything seems lost. Grace seems to have vanished. Heaven goes silent. Feelings disappear. Certainties collapse. Answers fade. What remains is an inner void, a vast nothingness, a silence that does not console, a sky without light. And yet... this is where trust is tested.

2. Trust Is Not a Feeling

Trust is not based on emotion or proof. It is a decision of the heart. To remain, not because you feel something, but because you know whom you love. When nothing is seen, yet you still whisper "I trust You, Lord," that is the beginning of real faith.

3. The Soul's Marriage to God in the Dark

Saint Symeon the New Theologian once said:

"My marriage to God took place in the darkness." The deepest bond with God does not form in the light of miracles, but in the dark night of trust. When your hands are empty, but your heart still stays.

4. Reason Questions – Trust Remains

Reason demands:

- Why doesn't God answer?

- Where is He?

- Why doesn't He support me like before? But trust responds:

- I do not know why. But I trust Him.

- I do not need signs. It is enough that He exists.

5. When Prayer Brings No Feeling

There are times when prayer brings no warmth. You go to church and feel nothing. You approach Holy Communion with a dry heart. And yet this is where your love is purified. Will you remain, not for what you receive, but for the One you love?

6. A Testimony from the Divine Liturgy

Once, during the Divine Liturgy, I felt nothing. My mind was distracted, my heart numb. Before me stood Christ in the Holy Chalice. And I thought: "What meaning is there in communing like this?" Then a quiet humility stirred within me: "Lord, I have nothing to bring You only my persistence in staying." And I received Communion not from feeling, but from trust.

7. Emptiness as a Place of Divine Work

The void is not absence. It is a workshop of grace. Just as wheat grows in the hidden darkness of soil, so trust is born in the darkness of silence. God works secretly, quietly, deeply. When all seems frozen, He is molding your soul.

8. Trust That Seeks Nothing in Return

The purest form of trust is one that asks for nothing. It does not complain. It does not bargain. It stays. It waits. It hopes. This is mature love: To wait for God, even if He doesn't come. To love Him, even when He is silent.

9. Dialogue of the Soul with God

- Lord, everything is gone. I have nothing.

- Now you can remain for Me

- not for My gifts.

- I feel empty..

- I will fill your emptiness when you stop asking and start loving.

- And if it never gets filled?

- Then you will have reached the purest relationship with Me

- not one of blessings, but of the Cross and love.

10. Prayer in the Hour of Emptiness

Lord, I do not ask You to fill my emptiness. I ask You to dwell within it. Let not my faith abandon me, even when all around me crumbles. Teach me to love You without holding You, to trust You without seeing You, to wait for You, even if You do not come.If this emptiness is Your way of teaching me, let it become sanctified. If Your silence is Your answer, let it become hope. Amen.

11. Concluding Word – Patristic Saying

"The greatest love is not abandoning Christ when the whole world has abandoned you—and even when it seems Christ Himself has left you." Saint Silouan the Athonite

CHAPTER 8

Presence Within Absence

"And behold, I am with you always, even to the end of the age."

— Matthew 28:20

1. The Soul's Cry

The soul often cries out:– "Where are You, Lord? I don't see You. I don't feel You. I don't hear You..."And God answers—not with a voice, but with something deeper than feeling: with Presence. A presence that cannot be explained. That cannot be proven. But never leaves.

2. Feeling Is Not Proof

You do not see Him. You do not hear Him. And yet... something holds you. It is not your strength. It is Him. His presence is not dependent on your capacity to feel. He is Present because He is God not because you are capable of perceiving Him.

3. A Presence That Cannot Be Explained

There are moments when everything within you is dark. When faith has faded, and prayer seems meaningless. And yet you are still here. That is not your doing. It is Him, silently sustaining you. His presence doesn't shout. But it never abandons.

4. Patristic Witness

Saint Isaac the Syrian says:

"Where you think God is silent, there He is holding you more than ever."

And Saint Symeon the New Theologian adds:

"I do not see You, Lord, but I am certain You see me and will not hand me over to myself."

His silence is not absence. It is a hidden protection.

5. A Soul's Testimony

A young woman once said to me:– "Father, I no longer pray. I can't. I've sunk too deep."And I replied:– "Yet something still keeps you speaking of Him. Can't you see? That's Him."It is not our words that unite us with Christ. It is the soul's refusal to forget whom it loves.

6. When You No Longer Pray, But Still Belong

There are days when you have no words. No prayer. No emotion. Yet deep within, there is still something that loves Him. And then He comes not because you called Him, but because He knows you need Him.

7. A Presence That Asks for No Space

Christ demands no space. He does not force His way in. He dwells silently within our darkness. He becomes Presence without requirements. He is here, even when not invited.

8. Theological Truth

Christ is with us, even when we are not with Him. His presence is not dependent on our awareness. He does not require reminders. He is the One Who Is. Always present. Always silent when He needs to be.Always working even in what feels like absence.

9. Dialogue of the Soul with God

- Lord, I don't feel You. Did You leave me?

- No, My child. I became silent so you could learn to hold Me without seeing Me.

- But I don't even have the strength to pray...

- That is why I am beside you. Because now you are not calling Me with words

- you carry Me as longing.

- Then why don't You let me feel You again?

- Because now your faith is being built on love, not emotion.

- Are You really here, even when I cannot recognize You?

- Yes. And even deeper. I am here when your soul cannot see Me, because now you are walking by faith, not by sight.

10. Prayer in Your Hidden Presence

Lord, I often don't feel You. I don't see You. It feels as though You've forgotten me...And yet, something whispers within me: "Do not be afraid. He is here."

I have no words, no strength, and little faith—but I cannot deny You. I carry You in my darkness like something precious I don't know how to hold.

Don't leave me. Or if You are hidden, let not my pain feel like abandonment. Be silence that holds me. Be presence that does not shout, but sustains.

Be that touch that comes when I no longer have the strength to ask for it. If You must remain silent, let Your silence give me life. If I cannot pray, let my weakness become a stairway for You to descend to me.

Thank You for being with me even when I am not with You. Amen.

11. Concluding Reflection

God's presence is not a matter of feeling. It is a fact of salvation. It is Christ's promise that cannot be broken:

"Behold, I am with you always..."

If your heart cannot feel Him, look at your persistence in seeking Him. If you have no strength left to pray, notice your silent longing that carries Him still.

Christ never truly departs. Sometimes, He hides so that you may learn to love Him not for the joy He gives, but for who He truly is. Not for His answers, but for the mystery of His Presence within His seeming absence.

CHAPTER 9

When the Cross Becomes a Prayer

"Do not fear the Cross; it is the one that will teach you to speak to God when all else falls silent."

– Saint Isaac the Syrian

1. The Cross Speaks Without Words

The Cross does not shout. It doesn't explain. It doesn't justify itself. It simply stands. And in its silence, it speaks louder than any voice.

When you suffer in silence, when you carry on without being seen, when you endure without asking for reward at that moment, your very being becomes a prayer. Not with words, but with presence.

2. The Cross Is Not Punishment, but Invitation

God does not give us the Cross to crush us. He offers it to us as a sacred invitation to enter into the deepest mystery of life: participation in His Passion and Glory.

It's not about paying a debt. It's about drawing near: Not with comfort, but with nails. Not with joy, but with trust.

3. Christ's Prayer on the Cross

His strongest prayer had no elaborate words. It held: Blood: because He paid with His very self. Forgiveness: "Father, forgive them..."– Thirst: "I thirst..." Surrender: "Into Your hands I commit My spirit..."

This is the prayer of the Cross not saying much, but giving everything.

4. The Saints: Prayer in the Flesh

Saint Symeon the New Theologian said:

"The crucified person no longer prays with words; he is the prayer."

And Saint Arsenius said:

"Do not seek words in your prayer. Become the prayer yourself..."

This is no exaggeration. It's the very mystery of holiness: A life that becomes doxology. Pain that becomes intercession.

5. A Testimony of Faith: Kyra-Katina

I remember an old woman, Kyra-Katina. She had been bedridden for years, her memory fading, her words weak. One day she said with tears:

- "I can't pray anymore, Father. I can't speak clearly, I can't even think straight."

And I replied:

- "Don't worry. You don't need to say a thing. You are the prayer. Every breath, every tear, every moment of your patience
- all rise to God like incense."

She cried. Not from sorrow

- but from freedom.

6. The Spiritual Theology of the Cross

There is no deeper union with Christ than sharing in His Cross. The Church doesn't only sing of the Resurrection. It also sings of Golgotha.

"Through the Cross, joy came to all the world."

In the theology of the Fathers, the crucified soul is the one who no longer demands anything but offers everything.

7. When Prayer Falls Silent

There are moments when no words come. No psalm, no phrase, not even a sigh. Just a deep need to whisper:

"You know, Lord..."

And He replies not with sound, but with Presence. He simply stands beside you. Just as He stood by His Mother beneath the Cross.

8. The Miracle of Endurance

It is no small thing to carry a cross and keep going. It's the greatest miracle.

The one who suffers and does not complain, who is wronged and does not retaliate, who is silent and does not blaspheme –is a living wonder.

No one may notice. But God sees. And finds rest there.

9. Dialogue Between the Soul and God

- Lord, I no longer have words to say to You.

- I had none either, when I was dying for you.

- I suffer in silence.

- That's when I hear you most clearly.

- What if I can no longer praise You?

- Then let your cross sing on your behalf.

- What if I fall?

- I will hold you with My pierced hands.

10. The Prayer of the Crucified

My Christ, Grant me the grace to carry my cross without shouting. Let my pain not be a cause for complaint, but a bridge that unites my being with Your Silence on Golgotha. Let my pain become prayer, my exhaustion turn into incense, my silence into a cry of love. Do not let me ask to come down. Only to finish it with You. Amen.

11. Final Saying

"Do not seek words in your prayer. Seek to become the prayer yourself, and God will understand you before you speak." – Saint Arsenius the Great

CHAPTER 10

The Resurrection Within the Silence

"And it was the Sabbath... and God was silent."
(Traditional phrase for Holy Saturday)

1. Silence Before Glory

Before the Resurrection, there is utter silence. Christ lies in the tomb. Heaven is still. Earth is still. Hearts are still. There is no light. No hope. No life. And yet that's where the Resurrection begins. In the deepest silence, the greatest life is born.

2. Resurrection Does Not Begin with Noise

Resurrection doesn't burst forth with fanfare. It begins inside, not outside. It is born in darkness, cultivated in the depths of the soul. It's not a change of circumstances – it's an opening of the heart. When you stop hoping to receive, and start loving without conditions.

3. The Mystery of Holy Saturday

Saint Epiphanius writes:

"Christ was silent and Hades trembled."

The greatest act of salvation was not accomplished through sound, but through silence. The silence of Christ made the foundations of Hades shake. That silence is not passive. It is creative, divine, full of power and light unborn.

4. Silence That Becomes Doxology

Saint Isaac the Syrian teaches:

"The silence that has settled in your soul will become a voice of praise when the hour of grace arrives."

Do not despise silence. It is the soil where Resurrection is sown. Grace does not always arrive with noise. Sometimes, it walks barefoot, like the soft light of dawn.

5. When Everything Feels Dead

There were times in my life when I felt "dead." No purpose, no fire, no joy. I whispered within:

"Nothing will shine again..."

And yet, days later, without understanding how, I found myself praying – not with words, but with stillness. A peace, inexplicable and gentle, came over me like soft morning light. And slowly...I came back to life.

6. Resurrection Begins When You Least Expect It

Nothing had changed around me. I had no answers, no solutions. But something inside me had shifted. Resurrection had begun. Not with celebration, but with silent peace.

This is how grace often comes: when you stop fighting for light and begin to embrace the darkness with trust.

7. When God Falls Silent

It's not easy to endure the silence of God. To speak to Him and hear no reply. To pray and feel nothing.

But that's when He is working the most deeply. As on Holy

Saturday. Outwardly, all seemed lost. But Christ was descending into Hades, raising the souls of the dead.

8. Dialogue Between the Soul and God

- Lord, will Resurrection ever come?
- It is already being born, right where you thought all was lost.
- I feel nothing...
- Life begins from death. Grace springs out of silence.
- What if I never rise again?
- I will raise you even from the grave.

9. The Hidden Victory

The greatest victories are often unseen. The soul that manages to smile in the darkness. To hope in emptiness. To remain faithful without proof. That soul has already risen. Even if they do not yet know it.

10. Prayer of Silent Resurrection

My Christ, Do not let me fear the night. Help me to believe in Your Silence. Raise me quietly. Build Resurrection within me, even when I am only trying to survive. Make my sorrow a spring, my pain a fruit, my dust a seed of life. If I cannot sing, send the angels to do it for me. And when I rise, may I meet You in the stillness, just as I met You in the dark of the Cross. Amen.

11. Final Saying

"Resurrection is not announced with voices; it is revealed where silence has learned to believe." – Saint Silouan the Athonite

CHAPTER 11

The Mother of the Pillow

1.   A Testimony, A Dialogue, A Prayer:

He never left me...

These are not the words of a book.

Not a theological analysis.

It is the voice of a mother, and behind her, the voice of thousands.

"These are the ones. This is the truth. I've lived it too..."

Simple words. But this is the truth of blood.

It is the voice of a heart that has passed through many nights,

that saw her child paralyzed in bed and did not bend.

"But in the end, I was not alone..."

Because He never leaves.

When all fall silent, He remains.

When hope withers, He breathes life.

When a mother cannot bear it anymore, He lifts her.

"I didn't ask for something else. He was already there.

God, always by my side..."

She didn't ask for what she thought she needed.

She received what she truly needed:

Strength. Patience. Light. Courage. Trust.

"I surrendered to Him... trustingly."

She didn't ask for the pain to go away.

She asked to go through it **with Him**.

That is the greatest faith:

Not to ask God to change your life

But to hand your life over to Him.

2. "And I said the things that wounded me... and like a great miracle, I saw them all in front of me."

Not because the situation changed —

But because God lit up her heart with meaning.

And that is the miracle:

Not that the child was healed

But that the mother became holy.

"In those difficult moments, He never left me..."

That's who God is.

He doesn't promise ease.

He promises Presence.

And when she stood by her daughter,

He stood by her.

"And I always glorify His Name!"

Because her gratitude is not about what she received

But that she was never alone.

Because **He was, is, and will be** even in the darkness.

3. Dialogue between Mother and God

- Lord... why doesn't my child walk?

- Because you entrusted her to a Cross that becomes a Holy Gift.

- Lord... why didn't You hear me when I cried all those endless nights?

- I did hear you. I just didn't speak

- because I was holding your hand.

- Lord... why are others healed, and not us?

- Because you are already healing the world with the light that your patience shines.

- Lord... didn't You grow tired of seeing me cry?

- No. Because your tears water Paradise.

- Lord... if I had another life, I wouldn't want it like this...

- And yet, you turned it into light.

Your daughter became a holy iconostasis.

- Only You remained...

- I was always there.

4. Prayer for Mothers who Carry a Cross

Lord, cover them...

Cover these mothers who do not sleep at night,

who hold not just broken bodies,

but wounded souls in their arms

dependent, paralyzed, suffering.

Give strength to those who carry their Golgotha at the pillow.

To those who never cried out loud,

who never complained,

who never said "why me,"

but whispered:

"Lord, help me to love."

Give their weariness the fragrance of grace.

Turn their tears into eternal fruit.

And when their hour comes,

do not judge them by deeds or numbers,

but by one small thing:

"I never left my child or You."

Let that be their gate into Paradise.

5. Mother–Daughter Dialogue

Daughter (Elisavet):

Mom... I heard you.

Even when everyone thought I couldn't speak.

Every time you cried silently beside me,

your tear touched me deeper than needles.

Mother (Dimitra):

I saw nothing, my child...

I only said your name.

I held the icon of the Virgin close.

And I told Her:

"I don't ask for anything... just her breath."

Daughter:

I remember that night.

I had said to the Virgin:

"I am small. I want to live..."

And She didn't turn Her back. She came.

She stood by my bed.

And to my left... angels.

Mother:

When you told me, I thought I was dreaming.

But deep inside, I already knew.

Daughter:

You never asked "why."

You never screamed to heaven.

You only said:

"Virgin Mary, You know..."

And every time I was in pain, I heard you whisper:

"Prayer, my daughter... That's our medicine."

Mother:

My child, I don't know if you'll ever get well.

But I see you live and smile through the Cross.

Turning pain into prayer.

And I say:

"This is my miracle."

Daughter:

Do you remember what I said when you hugged me again?

"I want daddy to take me to the Virgin.

To light a candle. To raise my hand..."

I still want it.

Mother:

He will, my child

When She says "now,"

She will lift you not I, not the doctors.

She has held you from the beginning.

Daughter:

I'm not afraid anymore.

As long as She's here, and you're by my side... I'm okay.

Even if I hurt.

Mother:

Me too, child... me too.

We are together, in Her shadow.

And that's enough to keep going.

The Embrace to the Virgin Mary – Mother, Daughter, Father**

Daughter:

Mom... I didn't tell you again:

I want daddy to hug me and take me to Her icon.

To light a candle. To say thank you.

Mother:

I know, my child. I held it in my heart all these years.

And daddy is waiting.

He always says:

"When She asks me for her again,

will take her just like when she was little…"

Father (softly):

Elisavet… I remember when you were a baby,

how I held you while you slept…

Now I want to lift you again

Not because you grew up,

but because you believed.

Because you endured.

Daughter:

Daddy… will you take me there?

In front of Her icon? Just for a little while.

To say thank you.

Not because She healed me

But because She kept me alive.

Prayer of Elisavet to the Virgin Mary

My Panagia…

I don't know why You kept me.

I only know You were there.

At my bedside. In my mother's tears.

And I thank You.

I ask You for nothing, not health, not strength.

Just one thing:

Don't leave me.

When I'm in pain, remember me.

When my mother cries, warm her heart.

And when the day comes when I can walk again toward Your icon, place joy in my soul and light in my path.

I don't have much to say...

Just one candle.

And one heart that loves You.

Hold me.

Like then.

Like always.

Amen.

A Letter from a Mother to the Author

Dear Fr. Christodoulos,

Thank you deeply for the honor you gave us by including our cross in your book.

I pray that many souls may find comfort in it.

I humbly share my personal experience exactly as I lived it.

It was the eve of the Virgin Mary's feast day...

The small hospital chapel was celebrating.

I stood before Her icon with nothing to ask for, only tears and a kneeling heart.

My tears soaked the floor.

And with all the strength my soul had, I told Her:

"Panagia, I ask nothing for myself.

I have an eighteen-year-old child... Give her Your breath. That's all."

She... asked for it herself.

She said with tears:

"Panagia, I am small... I want to live. Give me Your breath..."

From that moment on, a long road began for us, a struggle to stay alive.

Prayer became our breath.

Faith, our nourishment.

The icon of the Virgin, our support.

I never asked for anything.

Only forgiveness.

And gratitude.

And I always tell Her:

"Panagia, You know what is best for her.

You hold her in Your hands..."

Elisavet has now lived for twenty years in a way that doctors cannot explain.

But faith holds her.

The Virgin Mary never left us.

And I, without ever complaining,

without ever saying "why me,"

carry my cross with love.

Prayer became my medicine.

The Virgin, my path.

The miracle is our daily life.

Just a few nights ago, during a vigil,

I stood again before Her icon.

I didn't ask Her for anything.

Only tears... and thanksgiving

for all She has granted us.

When the accident happened,

Elisavet could still speak.

She asked for an icon of the Virgin.

All night long, she prayed:

"Our Father...

And when the doctors came to intubate her,

her last words were:

"Panagia, into Your hands I give my soul."

Since that moment, she has been intubated for a month.

And when she woke up, she said:

"Mama, the Virgin was at my bed.

And beside my head, right and left, were angels watching

over me."

Her only wish when she gets better is this:

"To have daddy hug me and take me to the Virgin.

To light a candle..."

This is our story.

Not a tragedy.

Not a mourning.

But a miracle of faith

that continues every day

within the light of the Virgin Mary.

Dedicated to E.

To you, a discreet and luminous soul,

who stood beside me when everything was fading;

who did not rush to rescue me with words,

but remained like a silent prayer at my side.

You taught me that ashes are not the end,

but the soil where God's seed takes root;

that pain, when surrendered,

can become a hidden bridge for another's healing.

I owe you not only support,

but revelation:

that the cross I bore was not in vain,

but a prelude to Resurrection for others.

If these words offer comfort,

it is because you once comforted me —

not with many words,

but simply with your presence.

Epilogue

If You've Made It This Far...If you've made it this far, perhaps a certain silence has touched you. Maybe you, too, have felt that emptiness that cannot be filled, that darkness that defies explanation, that silence of God which, rather than wounding, gives birth to faith. I did not write this book to teach you. Nor to give you answers. I wrote it to kneel beside you. To sit in the silence with you and say: You are not alone. God hears you, even when He is silent. He sees you, even when you can't see Him. And He is preparing a Resurrection, still hidden from your eyes, but more certain than light itself. Hold your cross a little longer. Remain in this silence just a little more. And when the time is right, you will see Him rise also within you.

Final Prayer My Christ, Thank You for the things I never understood, for the questions You never answered, for the knots You never untied. Thank You, because within Your** Silence, my own prayer was born. And if one day I fall completely silent, may my very being rise up to You like incense to the One who sees what is hidden.Amen**